The Knotting Poems

SELECTED OTHER BOOKS BY MARTIN BOOTH

POETRY
The Crying Embers (1971)
Coronis (1973)
Snath (1975)
The Knotting Sequence (1977)
Extending Upon the Kingdom (1977)
Devil's Wine (1980)
The Cnot Dialogues (1981)
Meeting the Snowy North Again (1982)
Killing the Moscs (1985)

AS EDITOR
James Elroy Flecker, Unpublished Poems and Drafts (1971)
The Book of Cats (1977) (with George MacBeth)
Contemporary British and North American Verse (1984)
Aleister Crowley: Selected Poems (1986)

NON-FICTION
British Poetry 1964 to 1984: Driving Through the Barricades (1985)
Carpet Sahib, A Life of Jim Corbett (1986)
Rhino Road: The Black and White Rhinos of Africa (1992)
Opium: A History (1996)
Doctor and the Detective—a Biography of Sir Arthur Conan Doyle (1997)
Magick Life: A Biography of Aleister Crowley (2000)
The Dragon Syndicates: The Global Phenomenon of the Triads (2000)
Cannabis: A History (2003)
Gweilo: Memoirs of a Hong Kong Childhood (2004) [US title: *Golden Boy*]

FICTION
Hiroshima Joe (1985)
The Jade Pavilion (1987)
Black Chameleon (1988)
Dreaming of Samarkand (1989)
A Very Private Gentleman (1990)
The Humble Disciple (1992)
The Iron Tree (1993)
Toys of Glass (1995)
Adrift in the Oceans of Mercy (1996)
The Industry of Souls (1998)
Islands of Silence (2002)

Martin Booth

The Knotting Poems

Shearsman Library

First single-volume edition.
Published in the United Kingdom in 2018 by
Shearsman Library
an imprint of Shearsman Books
50 Westons Hill Drive
Emersons Green
BRISTOL
BS16 7DF

Shearsman Books Ltd Registered Office
30–31 St. James Place, Mangotsfield, Bristol BS16 9JB
(this address not for correspondence)

www.shearsman.com

ISBN 978-1-84861-595-3

Copyright © Martin Booth, 1977, 1981.
This edition copyright © The Estate of Martin Booth, 2018.

The right of Martin Booth to be identified as the author of this work
has been asserted by his Estate in accordance with the
Copyrights, Designs and Patents Act of 1988.
All rights reserved.

ACKNOWLEDGEMENTS
The Knotting Sequence was first published in 1977 by
The Elizabeth Press, New Rochelle, NY;
The Cnot Dialogues was first published by the same press in 1981.

Contents

The Knotting Sequence / 7

The Cnot Dialogues / 67

The Knotting Sequence

for Jim and Norb & Katherine
who flew me

NAMING THE PLACE

Chenotinga
Cnottinga
Gnottinge
Knotyng
Knottinge
Knotting

they have called
this the
Place of
the Sons
of
Cnot

INSTRUCTIONS TO NEW WORLD READERS

52°. 15'. 40"
North

0°. 31'. 45"
West

a row
of dying
elms

the crack
of frost

the cry
of lapwings

Knotting

at last a
place with no
enemies

said Cnot settling
there, unaware
of the sun's
bite and the
moon's pull and
the snow

in the name of
Offa

in the name of
Arthur

in the name of William
of Normandy

in the name of
Henry
John
Coeur de Lion
Victoria

I declare these
fields
royal

no screams the
dead Cnot

these blades
of grass
are *ours*

THE TOADSTOOL

livid, white
in the brown,
busted earth

see it
raise its
ugly, venereal
head

phallus
impudicus

Cnot's rude
jest

potsherds
> beads

a knife-blade
> stones

bones
> a clay ball

I wish
there was a
way,
Cnot,
for you to
send to
me a

portrait

peace
is Cnot's field

quiet
is Cnot's field

soft
is snowfall
is Cnot's field

green
is Cnot's field

red berries
is Cnot's field

wind-strewn grass
and birdsong
is Cnot's field

you've
just
been

there

NOISES FROM THE WOLD

who owns those screams?
who lives to scream so?
who dies in such
screaming?

not the trees
not the birds
not the voles and squirrels
not the dumb adders
not the licentious frogs
not even
the snared
and howling
hares

only one
can scream
so, said
Cnot

not I
not I
not I

he counted his
sons and daughters
and brothers and sisters and wives
and dogs

all correct

but some-
one was
screaming

in the forest
Cnot tried
screams

he howled
and the wolves answered

he twisted his flesh
and the snake loved him

he caterwauled
and the echo returned
to crawl into his mouth

and die

whatever
it was
it was not
the scream of a pulled grass stem
or the jay's mimickry

Cnot drew
closer to the sound of pain

over it
and through it
he placed
a newer
noise

a grunt
a groan
a moan
a bellowed sigh

not a boar
not a lame man lifting a log
not a lover
with his joined groin
and the release
of life

Cnot peered
over the chaos
of bushes

it is said that
in the field above the
church in nearby
Yelden there
was fought a
skirmish between the
local Belgae and
a small unit of the
Roman occupation
force sometime in
the last two
decades of the first
century AD   an
arrowhead of bronze was
discovered when grave-
digging in the last
century   the local
tribe were resoundingly
defeated.

I remember *that*
Cnot says

I didn't go
to help

no sense drawing
them over here

he counted his
wives again and
a new
moaning washed
across the evening

we don't
really need
this holy
building
(said Cnot as
they felled the
elms for
the first
nave)

we don't
really need
this holy
building
(said Cnot as
they cut the
first stone for
the second
nave)

we don't
really need
this holy
building
(said Cnot as
they carved the
first gargoyle for
the new
nave)

we don't
really need
this holy
building
(said Cnot

converted to
Jesu
in seventeen-thirteen,
after a thousand
years of
waiting upon
the left
hand)

we have a
god-place
built by
god
already

(he spanned
the fields with
two
wide fingers)

COMPLAINT

it is
all your
fault that
the lane
twists

you had to
insist on
building your
hovel so
I have to
slow the
car down for
a tight
corner

hovel!
(hear him bellow?)

hovel,
my arse!

this is my
home

that whisper you
hear when
the power-brakes
bite is
wind
in my thatch

so turn
damn your
eyes

remember: you
share this
place with

me

"heaven is full of fools who had
too many prayers granted"

Cnot seldom
prayed — that's
why he is
still here

minding
his own
business

AN APOLOGY

I am
sorry for
bringing tame
roses into
a field of
spotted
orchids

I am
sorry I
dug the land

I am
sorry the
hedge has been
trimmed

I love
you, Cnot

but this
order is
part of — me!

LETTER TO CNOT FROM THE POET IN NEW YORK CITY

Cnot:

I write to
say I'm in
the promised land

the houses pile
into the clouds

the cars are
gold and red

the sirens — well,
they weep out
sound

the streets are
known to *breathe*

ah! says
Cnot, cynic

now tell
me you've
met
god

POSTCARD TO CNOT FROM THE USA AFTER THE PREVIOUS LETTER

don't be so
jealous, Cnot, you
old bastard

so:
I'm going to
America

so
what

here in
NYC I
eat my
supper, but
my watch
says
01:40
(and the next
date, too)

what more
do you want

love?

the wind
runs over the
high, blonde
corn like
fingers over a
hand
of cards

Cnot
plays on

deals
another one
of those personal
trumps

the wind
runs over
the high summer's
barley

and
i can't
win a
trick

THE BLASPHEMERS
for John

how we
blasphemed
that day

drunk on
retsina we
laughed like
hell under the
ghost-shadow of
the willow

and, god let
us go! We
sand Greek
songs where
Icelandic should
have been

we christened this
house, this
place with wine

Cnot
lying in fields
demanded
mead

over the green
life of the grass

burns the raucous
yellow flight of
a brimstone, its
antennae knowing
where the Blue Moon
roses are

all that's left
of Cnot's anger

to the eye

CNOT CHASTISES BAD SHOOTING

missed a
hare again on
friday: worth
seventy-
five pence in
the butchers'

Cnot huffs

seventy-
five pence!
seventy-
five pence!

worth a
full belly in
January, salted

or
a glorious gut-
ache on
Tuesday

pass
the fire!

in Bletsoe
Close on
Sunday I
found another
Avon cannon
shell

and
live

that's the
third

above ghosts
chase the
Luftwaffe
off
Cnot's
fields

the frost at
first light is
as thick
and fine as
snow

this is
how one
knows Cnot
is near

to make
frost one
must have
vapour,

breath
even

TESTIMONIAL

this, Cnot
is my
dog, Chester

he is
dead

recognise his
stillness, lips
drawn in a
smile (like
yours) born
of a full
contentment

he has
been — as
you know — a
companion of
hedgerows and
sunsets

his undivided
love has
been mine even
when I've
only just
beaten the
old bugger

he joins
you

I commend
him to
your ancient
hearth

I beg
you love
him by
proxy until
I join
you a hundred
metres from
here
and feed
him more
of the bones he
always found in
furrows and
ditches

yours

the curtains gently
billow their
buff skein hung
between
the grey morning and
me

who pushes them
out like
cheeks?

Cnot?

Cnot!

GUIDE TO THE METAPHYSICAL ANATOMY OF CNOT, SONS OF KINGS, LORD AND WORSHIPPER

winter elms'
shadows cast
by a
full November
moon

the lines
of Cnot's
palms upon
the roadway

sheened ice
upon
the field puddles

Cnot's eyes

the hollows of
dead thrushes'
nests
— possibly

Cnot's
ears listening to
nightfall

no smell
or
touch

these few
I'll lend
to you

forefather Cnot

Ted can
recall the
days and
nights of the
lambing, a
time when
ewes' bleating
filled Old
Blackwells

Cnot on
the other
hand recalls
his first
son's belch of
purple blood
as his first
wife
died

sorrow's
a marriage of
good and
sad he
said

to Boda

THE STONE BEAD

found
it when
shooting
rabbits

dropped
the mauve
cartridge

picked
up the
stone nativity
of the bead

pushed
the mud
out of its
hole with
a twig

shrugged
off time
easily

EXTRACT OF A LETTER FROM ARCHBISHOP LAUD TO REV. ARTHUR ALVEY

and I do charge that
you — Arthur Alvey — did
on Shrove Tuesday in
the year of our
Lord sixteen
hundred and thirty-
six commit the
sin against Jesu
Christus, our
Master, in that you
did with knowing
hand concede to
the exhibition of
fighting cocks in
the chancel of
the Holy Church of
St Margaret of
Antioch in
the parish of
Knotting, for which
unlawful and
blasphemous sin you
shall hereby be
cast from the sight of
the Lord.

the candle dies
love dies

each Sunday, my
wife and I close
the door on Arthur's
fighting cockerels

THE PULPIT

beetle-ridden, it
lurches

the pews are
black with age

under the
centre
beam, Bunyan
sang

for sure

where
the well stood:

where
the old school stood:

where
the lane began:

where
the pump rocked:

this is
where they
say she
sings

a washer-
woman, who
longs to taste
her husband

lost
(she sings)
in Flanders

dawn here is
not the sight
of a grey slip
of day
over a far
spire — it's
the weeping
mew of
hen pheasants in
the greying
stubble

awoke at
six

bearing
eight bronze
bruises in
my left
shoulder by

eight dead
rabbits
in the
porch

eight bloods
mingling
with dreams

doves
wing into
the trees

wind
is caught
in them

NOVEMBER, HERE

mist at
dawn: damp
hair and
cobwebs

love of the sun

now
the Fiat
won't start

who cares
that sings?

suddenly

far

off

the

clichéd
clack of

ducks

'not
indigenous'

is a
cruel way to
speak of
those short-
horned little
enemies of tree-
bark

who stutter and
cough though
the dusk

barking deer some
rich bastard stole
from China

two centuries
ago

seedy sycamores
drop wings
into the water

there
to fly
upon their own

reflections

at last!

a peregrine
nesting in
the old
barn's oak

new blood
to be spilled
next autumn

out of the
standing
corn Charlie takes
it easy: over
the banked
stubble he
sort-of runs a
steady trot

we 'coarse
bastards' (he
thinks in fox-
Latin or fox-
Greek) whistle and
hoorah! at him

by the hidden
pond under the
willows he
pauses: even
at a distance of
300 yds. his
triumphant grin's
complete

did you (breath-
less) see his
mask? Christ,
that was a fine,
fine dogfox

on the
cornice of the
church's buff-
stone tower a
Little Owl squats

guarding its
eyes against
the sun and
the hedgecutters

it knows that
up there
we can't reach
even with
moralities

more dead
leaves from the
hawthorn

broken
petals upon
the lawn

snapped
rat in
the trap

a gentle
twitch of
feather

the dry-
ing of Grit
Pond

last wind-
falls of
apples in
the shadows

all this

I speak of
yesterday

in Raven's
Oak
the pimpernels
are blushing

sunset
is
shameless
over them

sitting here, a
bourbon laps the
ice around:

sitting here, five
miles over
Salzburg, staring
at Berchtesgaden

sitting here, the
blizzards tearing at
Vienna Airport

sitting here, I
— lone flyer
and lone
angel — dream
of the ash
we planted
seven days
ago

in every
leaf of the
silver birch

is a silver
hand longing
to clap

is a silver
mouth longing
to sing

is a silver
coin longing
to buy

silence

pigeons' wings
clap above
the furrows

the white wing-
bands
flash — this
is a
warning they
all know

this is
summer's
applause

question: what
disgrace of
beauty suggested to
the Eastern
Electricity Generating
Board, to
erect a grey
relay transmitter
box upon
a stiffened
pine pole in
a direct
line between my
study and
the histories held with-
in the
church-tower and
ten dying
elms
?

here am
I

over there is
a Caterpillar
tugging a disc-
harrow through
the loam

here am
I

hearing age and
the earth
rebel

August 17:
Stack Close — wheat

August 18:
Melchbourne Mead — wheat

August 19:
Grit Field, Wayposts — wheat
   & barley

August 19:
tonight at
seven as
light was leaning
down, the
end wall of
the long
barn fell out under
the weight
of heaped
grain

my lords of
earth; this
has been
a good
year

sit quietly

at the
window

dusk falls

the Bantams withdraw
into their
straw and
gloom

a leaf turns

no: is
turned

the teeth of the
trap close faster
than sight

blood
again

once
a land of
sixty
ponds and
springs

time and
tractors
filled them
in

now
the wheat
reflects
clouds

the power
saw screeches

whines

already we
are dreaming of
flames and
roast nuts

The Cnot Dialogues

*I only need the
god;
I do not need the
priest*

for my son Alexander

October has begun; the
day's been
keen and the wind's
straight off ice

blue today, a
joyous knot of
clouds: all
moving, three-
quarters of
a moon over the
shoulder of the
church

wore gloves

in the peach of
dusk, waved too

such are
these dia-
logues

the fair
wheat eyes the
sky which
eyes the
wheat

the wild
oats sewn
by wind and
mostly dead in
the seed have
tiny black pigs'-
eyes

which dare
not even
look
you
or you
straight in
the face

Cnot looks
everything in
the face and
the seasons will
flourish all
the
better on it

you must hark
back, said
Cnot, drive back &
know: no

not in a
car — 'drive' in
that other sense, of
move and
be and
long to
be

the fun's
over, the
fireworks of
law and war and
instant electricity, is
done

seek the
flame in the head of
the snake: the burn
in the womb: the
wheeling of
seasons: why!
You've a
place here for
it

live for the
dead and
live

since Thursday's
light
fall of
snow filled
the deeper
furrows

and Friday's
sun
killed any
hint
of winter upon
the ridges

the earth has
been browned if
viewed over
the fields but
worried by
snow if viewed
along the
hedges

deceptive, this

a land that can
frown
in winter

walking up the
rise, some spring
mornings
the sky's so
clear you'd
think the
sea was only just
beyond
the trees

it has that some-
how glow; I
guess the strung-
out clouds
help, carrying
it inland

Cnot and the
others never
saw the sea

they doubt
these words

I keep it
secret from
them I can
fly

RABBIT, DEAD ON THE A6

in darkness, it
was done: a
thud was
all the owl or
rat had
known

later, as
the sun came
up, more ve-
hicles had
pulped it to
a stain upon
the A6, south
of
Rushden

only, propped
by splintered
bones, the
ears alone re-
mained, stood
up, split
apart by
air: and this
was its
curt, condemning,
crude and
final
gesture to
us
all

SADLY, GLADLY, NO PUNS

someone
is sure to come in the
room and snatch the
ball from his hands

someone
may even
kiss him and
his lips will grow
numb

someone
shall shout in his
face their spit rubbing
into his pupils

someone will shriek

someone
will guide him to a
long drop and help
him over

someone will even get him a
concrete overcoat

someone
will rat on
him, will fink on
him to the authorities

someone
will fool him with
love and
leave home laughing

someone
will steal his
watch and all his
time with it

someone will wonder about him
curiously

someone will take pains to
ignore him

   and it
   will come to
   pass that when
   he wakes the
   day will be
   normal save
   that no birds shall
   be singing

Cnot knows little of
this — he
was a
farmer

silence is not a thing to
treasure, though voice-
less nights are good

pause: if we
stop talking
now and there
is no
sound

how shall we
hear if the
wind blows cool or
warm, if
the rain
falls

(Cnot
snores)

this is how the
fire replenishes cold
stones

and the damp
worm is known to
squirm in the horror of
this dessicate
dryness of
what was alive

wood ash: coal
ash: flesh
ash (for I
throw bones from
the plates in to
crick in the
grate) they have
that singular familiarity with
deserts

under the apple, each
winter's morning, my
wife dumps the
fire's gurry and
the grey
rot blenches the
frost

    and
every spring, the
wet apples grope
toward the
bulk of the
summer's throat

dusk: and all
iced with
night, even
the just-full
moon

my black
boots brush the
white off
the trailing
grasses, the
rape leaves crisp and
brittle

hard, hoar-
frost for
five days
solid

the sharp
air sinks &
the west
darkening

then a cri.
ck.ck.ck.ck.
overhead

making for
the gravel
pit the raised
eyebrow-like
wings
of a late-
night
heron

my black
gun is
lowered: it's
all
a myth

DIGGING SALSIFY

the root slapped
up and the
dirt pucked
upon my blue
cuff

the sap
was in
it

the stain was
so red
went indoors
to see
if the cut
was deep or if
it was
another of
his rude
jests

as if the wind is
carrying some bright
spark chucked
up by
Cnot far
off they turn
their belly
feathers on or
off and on
again

the blacks of the
wings're invisible: their
eyes too
small

but the evening
sun, hanging
under the day's
storm clouds, catches
them

they wink
way over
Bottom Leys

the lying
straw's whet-
orange from
the rain

we can
see lapwings a
mile
off

cut not the last
sheaf: it must just
remain the winter
through, dressed in an
old hag's skirt and
shawl

which shall
be stripped
by the storms
of the winter's
vicious quarters and
the naked
dame (Cnot's old
mother? yes) 'll be
prepared, in rain &
April, for the
time of
her
life again

CNOT ATTENDS A RECORDING SESSION WITH A FEW OF THE POET'S FRIENDS

Cnot calls if
it is
rolling, Bob &
then he
wonders what all this futuristic
equipment is, with mixer-boards
and channel guides and fader
controls and tape decks and high
impedance microphones: it's
bunk, for
show says he

yet, when the
music starts and he
sees *real* humans out
there, cut
off from the
world by the
jangle of sound, the
song, the pain and the
pity

and he
hears it: then
it all makes
sense: as Aristotle once
whispered in
his ear
art is beyond and
like Chandler
said, we can live on
the edge of
nothing—

or
something real

it's in us
all

tonight, on Winter
Eve, a fierce-
some wind is
smashing every-
thing

the leaves will
all be
gone by
dawn: the
lawn flat, as
if a massive
hand had
been long sleeping there

the gate bangs &
the glass in
the study
window gives
in gives out gives
in enough
for the
hand that's
flesh to
know of it

one's hair's
like knotted
serpents after
a darking
walk

an appropriate
night for
the air's
indivisible snakes

all pictures must
first be
drawn and
all fields must
be sown
before you
eat

I suppose it's
in the
order of
things or the
gods would
smite it
down: cruel
they can
be

so reasons our
old ancestor as
he watches
the crop-
spraying aircraft bank &
turn for
another run in on
New
Ground

all winter, in
my study, over-
looking Cnot's own
garden and the
fields, behind the
pencil sketch by Lady
Caroline Lamb of
her son, I
reckon, hanging on
the wall by
the window, a
solid wedge of lady-
birds has lasted out
the cold wind and
the ice

at night, like
libertines, they come
out red and
strut or wing beneath
the reading
lamp: I take great
care to let
them not be rollered
flat within the
gears on my
humming type-
writer

they do me no
good yet no
harm

remind me that
summer's not a
myth

no, nor
is Cnot, the
sage who
stomps the
drifts of snow by
the letterbox: I
can't believe he
mails any
letters

he can't
write

and I
can't read, you hear
him bawl?

but I'
ve whittled
down more men than
you've writ
words

he's given to
exaggerate at
times

Cnot goes
off in a
huff

singing songs he's
learnt by
rote

an interlude:

Cnot sat quite
still by
his hearth, the
stones too
hot to
touch, the
woodsmoke punish-
ing his
eyes

& through the
tears he
watched that
year's first
snowflakes vanish
in his
flames

so far over the
tree line, it
hurt the neck to
look, it
stabbed: a
star is but one
of its many
possibilities

it flicked on,
off, on orange and
green and so
blue that it
might have been that of
which pain comes

it barely
moved: not an aircraft or
satellite, too high for a
helicopter

stood in the
field called Top
Leys in snow in
moonlight in minus
five centigrade and
watched it until winter drove
us in

later, it (what
-ever) made these
words

THE DEAL

furious he came
home from
the place where
they drop souls — &
screaming

masoned, dammit, and
in my own place, too

look at
this grain; ex-
changed for that
old cob that
went lame last
leaf-fall

chitted, bloody
shoots a-
greening in
my hand

masoned by that
bastard of
the big
head ley-
bound...

CHEATED!

strange verb, 'to
mason' (to
swindle in
horsedealing)

it's not I
who dare
it, Cnot

but I do know that
that old
horse could no
more pull
a plough as
pull a
docile
mare

squalid? never say
of twigs and
day that they
lack dignity

"this place has
atmosphere" says a
friend, buying the
next cottage

he'll
learn says
Cnot

it never
ceases:

autumn
means starlings massed &
squatting
on the 'phone
wires before
making it south to
Africa

Africa; what
does that
mean? asks
Cnot

prizes given for
the best
solution to
this puzzle

no more fine
cockbirds

no more fine
sunsets

no more fine
blood
running these
channels

yours or
yours

when you
go, go

when you
don't
go, don't
go

I couldn't
give a
tinker's curse

come, come; we
all know that
Cnot's as
prone to
lying as
the best
of us

the bell rings
seven in the
dying light

a firm
breeze dilutes
the penultimate
chime then
dies

the last's
a louder
bellow than
the others: Cnot
hears them
all

CNOT'S FEW WORDS TO ALEXANDER

listen, you
small, shagged-
out piece of
flesh called a new-
born son

do all
I say and
you'll not go
wrong

one; count frogs'-spawn
and wear the sticky
necklace at your
throat: two; touch only
inkcaps leaving to
stand the sickle-
tasters: three; bless
moths, kiss worms: four;
kill only that
you might eat or
yours: five; love the
rat who eats the
dead and succours
not the flies: six; seek
water: seven; prize
stones as if they
were the fingers of your
hand: eight; know how
the hares dance: nine;
take heed of the
wind: and ten; speak not
of this to cynical dis-
believers

in every grasshead, in
every one-legged
seed, in every squinnying
bud, I see
him

he believes living
is all

Cnot
rocks in the breeze with laughter
Cnot
's raucous in rain
Cnot
taps his fingers with the winter hail
Cnot
stands in the
sun turning
brown, turning to
god to
me

insidious pollens gather
in the pleats of
his coat and the
corners of
his eyes

motes
of gold
he watches, follows
me

and I him year
in year
out

PEEWITS

so silent, in their
clerical garb

like so many
solemn priests upon
a ritual
convocation

they nod and
bow, obsequious
as hell

usually noising by
now, they
make no
mew

showing now a
mourning for
her, for
Cnot and
all
time passed

this time to-
morrow, I'll be
in Chi-
cago

again? he
snickers, you
were only
over there last
year

dammit! isn't
this, my
hamlet, good
enough
for
you?

reply: of
course, it
is: you
know I
love the
place and
miss it

you curse the
mud — god
knows I'
ve heard
you oft enough
reply: that's
different, old
man

can't
you see that
hating is
as loving
does

I guess, he
says, I
guess

the church is timelessness itself and
every stone has locked up breath with-
in it longing to break free and
scour the yews that later came to hang
their deathly berries on the place

the clock has only one hand: the taxman
saw to that
and the windows are plain glass: the wars
saw to that
the tower leans a little to the west: the ground
saw to that
the roof's alack of pantiles: the January wind
saw to that
in '76

the fence has fallen: the sheep
saw to that
the walnut's gone: the axe and wedge
saw to that
the elms fell when the pantiles skimmed off
   the roof: the same storm
saw to that

life goes
on about
the place and
birds nest in
the eves: bats
hang in the
clockweight cup-
board: beetles
gnaw at the
rooftrees: moths

make arabesques about
the lights: mice
inhabit the table
tomb

Cnot
sees to that

on Sunday, I
sent Jim a
hare's front
paw

for luck

for luck? Jim
who?

you
know damn well!

ah, him
says
Cnot, the
other one who
spoke to
me and
smelt that
bloody dog-
fox in the
culvert
by the gravelpit

sod the
luck; send
him
my
love

quiz: which
is the
odd one
out?

pipperidge
cankers
feaberry
headache
haws
fat-hen

Coot thinks &
answers: fat-
hen

correct, say
I: that is the
only generic herbal
name in the
list

incorrect, growls
Cnot: we
never had fat
hens — ours
were always
scrawny little
buggers

now here's a
pretty thing, he
says, eye-
ing the cut
treestump by
the dog-
leg bend in the
lane

soon as I'
m turned you load of
shits cut
down the last
elm of
the row and I
was looking
forward to a
bit of
shade under
that come
August

we've tried, oh!
believe me, we've
tried but
old Cnot
won't
see that
the tree was
like him
dead

get
up, Cnot!

and he does
from the dark hollows in the
    oak's bark
or
the rabbit warren
or
the black pit of the owl's
    belly

and he
creeps up

everything agrees to sleep

this has
been going on
a long time

here

*carved on a
stone, under
an oak :*

*knock
not, for he is
absent*

*to return in
an aeon of
acorns*

AFT-WORD

a note for strangers to the place

Knotting is a hamlet of nine houses, a 1,200-year-old church and a few farm buildings: it is surrounded by fields of turned earth (in winter) and wafting wheat or barley (in summer), hedgerows and a few copses. It is also surrounded by Cnot, the archetypal ancestor, whose name (in Anglo-Saxon) is given to the place and who, at a multitude of levels, permeates the atmosphere of 'his' settlement, be it in the form of pot fragments (from pre-Roman to Victorian periods), field layouts or just the wind and the imagination. (Everyone leaves a mark-print where he's been—it's just that his is massive and wider reaching than, say, a footprint in the mud or dust.) To look upon an aged tree-stump, the churchyard wall or a dark mark in the earth (of a one-time ditch or pond) is to directly relate, communicate with those passed by. To speak is to let a stone hear now as it heard then ... dialogues through time with the gone. Not the dead: Cnot and those for whom he stands are not spirited away. They're still here. In the place. To love/know/hate/feel/recognise this (or any) place is to love/know/hate/feel/recognise them, the predecessors. Or him. Cnot—who is both man and earth, now and then, us. Appreciate him or them and we appreciate ourselves. It follows.

Publisher's Note

Since Martin Booth's death in 2004, nothing has been seen of his poetry and most of his novels have gone out of print, although—aided by the Anton Corbijn movie, with George Clooney in the lead role—*A Very Private Gentleman* did reappear, retitled *The American*. During the last 20 years of his life he was probably the writer I met most often, initially because of poetry and later because of his prose, which often used the Far East—where he was raised, and I was long resident—as a locus.

My connection with the Knotting books actually goes back further, to a friendship with James L. Weil (1929–2006), publisher of The Elizabeth Press from 1963–1981. The Elizabeth Press published mainly American poets—William Bronk, Cid Corman, John Perlman, Simon Perchik, John Taggart, Larry Eigner, among others—in fine letterpress editions, mostly produced on the presses of the Stamperia Valdonega in Verona. Jim gave me copies of these two books, along with many others over the years, and I think I'm right in saying that Martin was the only British author on the list. Jim tended to favour short-lined limpid poetry of the kind espoused by Cid Corman, although he was also a strong supporter of William Bronk's work, a more sonorous, longer-limbed kind of verse.

It's striking to me that Martin Booth's work in the two Knotting books slipped away from his normal British style into a more American, and indeed more *Elizabethan* form. By the time these books appeared, it was probably clear to Martin that he was not going to achieve a breakthrough with a major British poetry press: he had been around long enough, and had enough influential friends in the poetry world, that if he *was* going to be taken on by a major press, it would already have happened. He started moving into fiction, with the first two (later unacknowledged) novels appearing in the late '70s, and the breakthrough *Hiroshima Joe* appearing in 1985. The latter enabled him to retire from teaching to take up writing full-time, and he then produced a steady stream of fiction and non-fiction volumes: those who wish to follow these up would be best advised to try the aforementioned *Hiroshima Joe*, as well as *A Very Private Gentleman* (a.k.a. *The American*), *Industry of Souls* and *Islands of Silence*, the memoir *Gweilo* (titled *Golden Boy* for the U.S. market), and *The Dragon and the Pearl*, the best guide to Hong Kong that I have ever read. There are also some excellent books for children, with *Music on the Bamboo Radio* being especially worth reading.

The two Knotting books offered here together for the first time received minimal distribution in their first editions—especially the second volume, which appeared in a run of 250 copies and was issued right at the end of the Elizabeth Press' trajectory—and very, very few copies reached the U.K. It's a pity that more wasn't seen of them in their day. That said, when I look at them again, I suspect a little judicious editing would improve their chances, even now. However, in the absence of any indications from the late author as to how this might be best achieved, I have chosen to present the texts as they originally appeared—albeit also removing some blank pages that frankly looked like padding—a small *hommage* to two old friends, both publishers in their different ways (Martin also ran The Sceptre Press for many years, producing poetry chapbooks) whose shades I salute from this plane of existence while I still can.

Tony Frazer
Bristol
September 2018

www.ingramcontent.com/pod-product-compliance
Lightning Source LLC
Chambersburg PA
CBHW030906170426
43193CB00009BA/755